A DOG'S BODY

A DOG'S BODY

Joanna Cole

Photographs by Jim and Ann Monteith

William Morrow and Co., Inc. · New York

Printed in the United States of America.
2   3   4   5   6   7   8   9   10
Library of Congress Cataloging-in-Publication Data

Cole, Joanna.
A dog's body.
Summary: Describes the physical characteristics
and behavior of dogs stressing their relationship
to the wolf.
1. Dogs—Juvenile literature. [1. Dogs]
I. Monteith, Jim, ill.   II. Monteith, Ann, ill.
III. Title.
SF426.5.C637   1986   599.74'442   85-25885
ISBN 0-688-04153-1
ISBN 0-688-04154-X (lib. bdg.)

To Taffy and Muffy

What makes a dog a good pet? You can probably name a whole list of things: A dog will run alongside your bike or play tug-of-war. It will beg for part of your sandwich, guard your house, or just keep you company. Dogs make good pets because they are social animals—they like to be with others.

There are hundreds of kinds of dogs that all look different, yet scientists believe the ancestors of all dogs were wolves.

No one knows exactly how wolves were tamed by people. Maybe a pack of wolves joined a group of prehistoric hunters and gradually became tame. Maybe wolves came to human settlements looking for food. Or perhaps children adopted orphan wolf cubs for pets.

Over thousands of years, the offspring of these tame wolves became different from the wild ones. Their bodies became a little smaller; their jaws and teeth were less powerful; their coats took on different colors and patterns. They were becoming dogs as we know them today.

All dogs are descendents of wolves like these.

People knew that dogs with certain looks or abilities often passed these traits on to their puppies. So people learned to breed dogs for special qualities. For instance, people who wanted dogs to help them take care of their sheep would breed two dogs that were very good at herding. When the puppies grew up, the people would then breed the best herders in the litter. After many generations, the people had created a new type of dog that was excellent at herding sheep.

Other people bred large, fierce dogs for guarding, retrievers for hunting, even tiny lap dogs for pets. Today there are dogs of many sizes, shapes, and colors. Most of them don't look anything like wolves.

No matter what a dog looks like, its wolf ancestry has left its mark on the dog's body. Wolves hunt deer and caribou by chasing them over open land. Wolves are adapted for running.

Dogs are good runners, too. If you take a dog on a hike, it can run for hours. A dog's heart—large for its body size—pumps oxygen-rich blood to the muscles, giving the dog extra endurance. By comparison, a cat will tire on even a short walk. The cat's body is designed not to chase, but to wait and pounce on its prey, and a cat's heart is not as large for its body as a dog's is.

A walking animal, like a bear or a human, steps on the whole sole of its foot; a running animal walks on its toes. A dog's foot is actually made up of toe bones. The foot bones are elongated—lengthened—and the dog's heel is high up on the leg. The dog's legs are elongated, too. With its long legs, even a small dog has a long stride and can make good distance with every step.

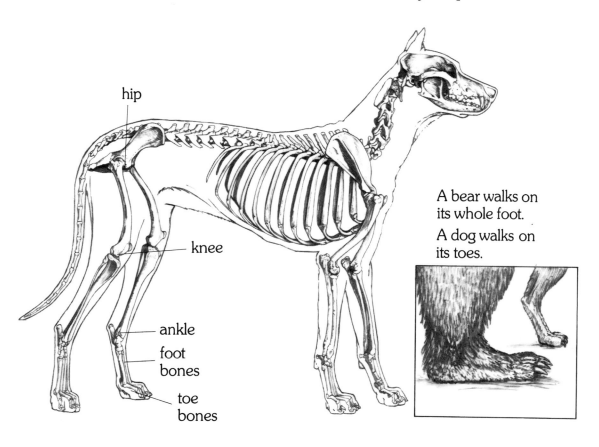

hip

knee

ankle

foot bones

toe bones

A bear walks on its whole foot.

A dog walks on its toes.

A dog's teeth and jaws are like a wolf's, except the dog's are a bit smaller and not as powerful. Both animals have tiny incisors at the front of the mouth for nibbling meat off bones and biting fleas. Four long, sharp teeth called canines are used for holding prey. And molars at the rear of the mouth that move across each other like the blades of scissors are for shearing flesh. Behind these, other molars are suited for crushing bones.

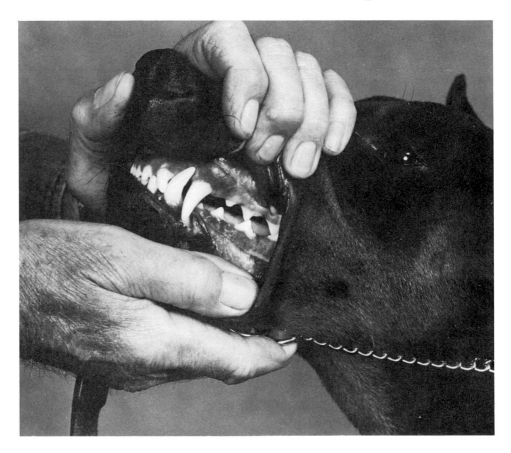

Dogs gulp their food without much chewing. This behavior is probably inherited from wolves. With many members of a pack all competing for a part of the kill, they "wolf" down their dinner. If a wolf or a dog wants to chew on a bone for a while, it carries it off to eat in private. This behavior prevents fighting over food.

Why does a dog pant when it is hot? Since dogs don't sweat (except in a small area between the toes), panting is the dog's way of cooling off.

A dog's panting looks simple, but it is actually a complicated process. It looks as if a panting dog is breathing in and out through its mouth. But it is really breathing *in* through its nose and *out* through its mouth.

Inside the dog's long nose is a maze of bones covered with moisture. Dry air coming in through the nose cools these bones by evaporation. When a breath of air has been in the nose for a second, that air gets hot. The dog then exhales this hot air through its mouth, which serves as an exhaust pipe. New cool air is taken in through the nose. Since all the blood in a dog's body passes through a special network of blood vessels between the nose and the brain, the dog's whole body is cooled by its nose.

When a dog pants:

cool air enters nose;   air cools area inside nose;   hot air leaves mouth.

When a dog's cooling system is working, its nose feels cold and wet. If a dog's nose is warm, people may think that the dog is sick, but this is not always true. A healthy dog often has a warm nose in cold weather or when it is at rest and does not need to cool off.

Like dogs, cats have few sweat glands and cool themselves by panting. But because cats are not running animals, they do not need a powerful cooling system. Therefore, cats' noses are shorter than most dogs'.

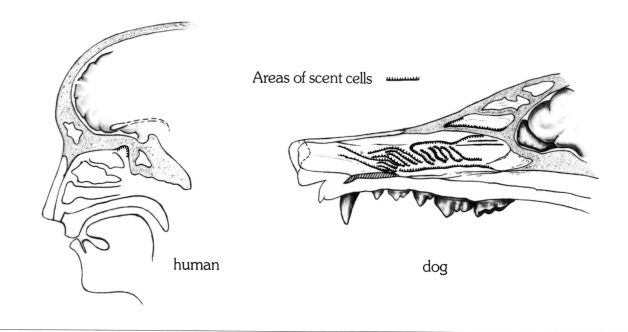

Areas of scent cells

human

dog

In a way, dogs live in a world that is quite different from ours. For example, a dog's world is full of information from smells that humans don't even know are there. Some dogs can detect the scent of a person's fingerprint six weeks after it was made!

The bones inside a dog's nose are covered with scent cells. This scent area in the dog's nose is many times larger than the scent area in a human's nose. In addition, the dog's brain has 200 million scent-receiving cells, compared with only 5 million such cells in the human brain.

It is not surprising that dogs are able to track missing people, to sniff out smuggled goods, and to locate gas leaks. Bloodhounds like this one are the best scenters in the dog world.

When I am at home with my dogs, they will often jump up and start barking "at nothing." Of course, they are not really barking for no reason. They hear something I cannot hear.

A dog can hear sounds that are four times farther away than those a person can hear. In addition, dogs can hear ultrasonic sounds—very high sounds—that humans cannot hear. This ability helps dogs hunt rodents, which often communicate with each other in ultrasonic squeaks.

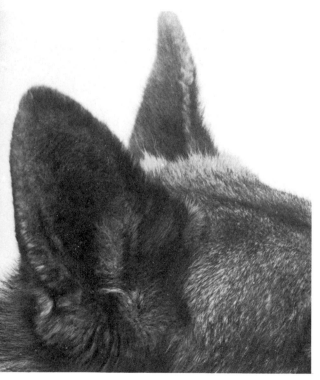 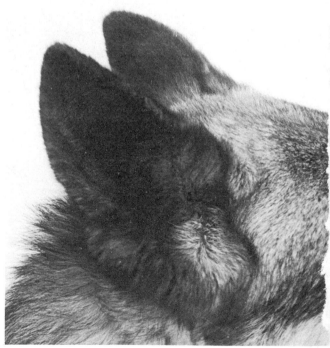

A dog tilts its head to locate a sound in front of it.

To pinpoint a sound, a dog uses its moveable ears. A dog has seventeen muscles for moving the ear; a human has only nine, and even these don't work very well. This explains why it is so hard for us to wiggle our ears.

The dog in the pictures on the left is locating a noise behind it. To zero in on a sound in front of it, a dog tilts its whole head. If you see a dog cocking its head near a clump of weeds, it is probably pinpointing a fieldmouse hidden there. Even without seeing the mouse, the dog knows exactly where it is—to the inch.

Dogs can smell and hear much better than humans can, but they cannot see better. Dogs probably see as well as a moderately nearsighted person without glasses—that is, dogs see the outline of shapes, but small details are blurry at a distance.

I know that my dogs rely more on their noses than their eyes. If I am walking toward a girl who is about the same age and size as my daughter, my dogs usually rush up to greet her. After sniffing, however, they realize their mistake and come running back.

People used to think dogs were completely color-blind, seeing the world in shades of black, white, and gray. Now we know that dogs *can* see some color, but it is difficult to train them to notice it. Color just does not seem very important to dogs.

Dogs' ancestors hunted mammals—deer, rabbits, mice—that are drab in color. For this kind of hunting, detecting movement is more important than seeing colors or fine details.

24

Unlike humans, whose sense of touch is located mainly in the hands and fingers, dogs touch mostly with the whiskers on the chin, muzzle, and cheeks. These hairs are connected to bundles of nerves. When a dog is eating, it cannot see a piece of food under its chin. The sensitive whiskers guide the dog when it is eating or when it is walking through narrow places in the dark.

How intelligent are dogs? Dogs are good observers, they notice things. They also have good memories. Years later, a dog may remember a place where it had a good—or bad—experience.

In general, dogs will repeat an action when they are rewarded for it. For instance, a dog that gets a treat for sitting up will learn to do that trick on command. A dog that once scratched on the door and was then let outdoors, quickly learns to scratch when it wants out. In the same way, a dog that rattled its dish by accident will learn to rattle it on purpose if someone usually responds by filling the dish.

Dogs do not have as large an area in the brain for reasoning and problem solving as do apes and humans. Therefore, dogs learn mostly through reward and punishment, rather than by imitating others or by puzzling things out.

Even so, dogs can learn complex skills. For instance, guide dogs for the blind learn to stop at every curb, to pick up dropped objects, and to lead their owners around obstacles. Most important, guide dogs learn *not to obey every command:* If there is danger, such as an oncoming car or a deep ditch, the dog must not go forward, even if its owner commands it to do so.

Because dogs are social animals, they have the ability to communicate with others. Like wolves, they "talk" to each other through facial expressions, body language, sounds, and scents. If you can read your dog's body language, you will understand your dog better.

Usually, a dog's lips are darker than the rest of its face. Sometimes the tips of its ears are darker, too. This makes the dog's expressions easier for others to see.

A friendly dog keeps its ears forward and its tail up, usually wagging. A happy dog will actually smile, turning up the corners of its mouth.

A playful dog often lowers the front half of its body and rests its forelegs on the ground. At the same time, it raises its rump in the air and wags its tail wildly, inviting you to play.

An angry, aggressive dog lowers its tail a bit, bares its teeth, and gives a warning growl, while the hairs on its neck and back may rise. This German shepherd is being trained by two policemen to attack on command.

A frightened dog lowers its tail still more, often tucking it between the hind legs. Its ears are laid back, and the dog may lie down or roll over to show that it will not fight.

It is *never* a good idea to pet a strange dog, even one that *seems* friendly. But it is especially dangerous to approach a frightened dog. Scared dogs may bite to defend themselves. Here are some rules for reading a dog's mood:

- The higher the ears and tail, the happier the dog is.
- The lower the ears and tail, the more frightened the dog is.
- The more teeth you can see, the more careful you should be.

In addition to body language, dogs communicate through sounds. Most of their sounds are the same as wolves': howling, growling, yelping, and whining. However, barking is one sound dogs make that wolves rarely do. Barking is a general sign of alertness. It warns others—dogs and humans—that something new is in the surroundings.

If a dog gives a high, shrill bark, it is a sign of fear. By contrast, a low, hollow bark shows aggression.

Even very young dogs seem able to understand the differences between barks. Our new puppy jumped into my arms in fear when she heard the deep, hollow bark of a big dog nearby.

Humans can learn to read a dog's sounds, gestures, and expressions, but we can never learn the other important way dogs communicate: the language of scent. This is because our noses can't pick up the tiny traces of odors given off by scent glands near a dog's tail and between its toes. Other dogs can tell the sex, age, and even the mood of a dog by its scent. They also can tell if a female dog is ready to mate.

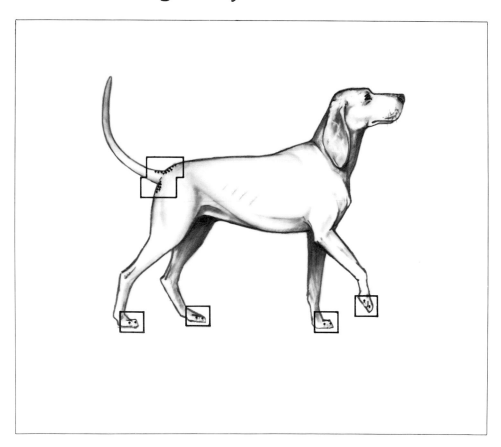

A dog's life as a social animal begins at birth. It is born into a ready-made pack, since there are usually three to ten, or more, puppies in a litter.

At first the puppies depend on the mother dog for warmth, care, and milk. Newborn puppies need body contact or their temperature will drop dangerously. To keep warm, very young puppies burrow over each other in a heap.

The face of a very young puppy has a blank look. Before puppies are two weeks old, they have almost no facial expression and do not wag their tails.

By about three weeks old, puppies start learning to communicate with others. Their faces become expressive and their tails start wagging. Humans respond to these signals as well as dogs, and it is at this age when puppies begin to seem irresistibly cute.

After three or four weeks, the puppies start eating solid food, and they suckle less. Now the mother dog spends more time away from the litter.

When she returns, the puppies may greet their mother by licking her mouth. In response to their licking, she may bring up some partly digested food, which the puppies eat. This is how adult wolves feed cubs that are too young to hunt.

Older puppies sleep side by side rather than in a heap. And they spend most of their waking time exploring and playing with each other.

Puppies learn a great deal by playing with each other. They learn to "read" each other's body language, and they practice fighting and hunting skills. They growl fiercely and even bite, but if their playmate yelps, they let up. Playful puppies hardly ever hurt each other.

If puppies have contact with people, they easily transfer their social behavior to humans.

Perhaps people and dogs get along so well because they have a lot in common. After all, our human ancestors were hunters who lived in groups, just as dogs' ancestors were.

People who don't know better may think of wolves as "wicked" animals, perhaps because they are presented that way in fairy tales. But it is the many ways in which dogs are like wolves that make people love dogs so much.